Dear Sophie

May this book b[e]
with love, magic & Inspirati[on]
for you & your amazing
Kitchen creations.
Greatest Gratitude
love & hugs
Natasha

Acknowledgements

My heart is filled with so much gratitude for all the help, patience and love from others who have sat, held space, encouraged and supported this book, that became so much out of my comfort zone, for without everyone, the book would only have ever been a dream.

For Sammuel, my partner for his big golden heart filled with so much love, support and forgiving me when things got tough, and sharing your presence and pureness with me.
For helping make dreams come true.

For Gareth Stubbs, one of my best friends, for all your understanding, dedication, guidance, perseverance and love while making sense of all the challenges and early morning conversations. For taking me out of my own way so others experience the kitchen creations.

For John Martin for your friendship, all your loyalty, dedication, suggestions and attention to the detail of everything, for shining your light as you grow on your journey and getting out of your comfort zones, for trusting the process, so we can all grow together.

For Illa and Jeetu khagram, dear friends and teachers, for all your unconditional love, support, guidance, forgiveness and for belief that magic does happen and never giving up on me. For your gentle pushes and nurturing to find my life's purpose. For always lighting up the path of life that we walk along together.

For Master Zhi Gang Sha, world renowned Grand Master Teacher, Author, Humanitarian, for all your unconditional love, teachings, tools and techniques that you share for self healing and holding all of us with your big golden heart.

For all the spiritual and higher worlds, Kuan Yin, Mother Earth, stars, planets and galaxies who provide so much of what we don't see to the naked eye - for providing the vision, the groundedness and wrapping your compassion and love around us all as we work as one.

Words really are not enough
Thank you x

All rights reserved. No portion of this book may be reproduced, copied, distributed or adapted in any way, with the exception of certain activities permitted by applicable copyright laws, such as brief quotations in the context of a review or academic work. For permission to publish, distribute or otherwise reproduce this work, please contact the author Natasha@thelovingchef.co.uk

Forward

For our beloved friend who we have known for over 15 years, we just want to say how pride we are that this recipe book has finally been created so that other people can truly experience who
' Natasha - The Loving Chef ' is.

The Loving Chef is such an apt a title for Natasha. The heart is all about love & there has never been a second, a moment or a day where Natasha has not considered other people around her. She is someone who has a heart of gold, & shines that heart of gold onto every word, & every recipe within this book. Her love flows out into everything that she is doing & does for the world.

After personally tasting many of Natasha's dishes, we can honestly tell you there is not one recipe that we have experienced that has not been created without her heartfelt love & passion to create a Vegan, Gluten-Free, Sugar-Free dish that not only nourishes our bodies & souls, but also help move us towards a more sustainable path for our planet.

We so dearly wish you to experience these recipes, experience this love that has been poured into creating this book for you all.

Thank you, Natasha, for all that you do, for everything that you are, for the healing that you give to the world through not only your food but your beingness of who you are. Thank you for the service you have offered to not only the people around you but to the people who may never do anything for you, the homeless, the people who are living hand to mouth every day.

We feel so privileged to be by your side, to experience & watch your confidence grow from within & we are so proud, & honoured to be able to call you our friend & much more.

Natasha Caton, the world needs more of you & the world needs to experience the love, the compassion, the light that you give out to everyone. Thank you for putting a part of YOU into this book so that others can experience The Loving Chef as we have done.

We wish you the greatest success & for anyone who experiences
your recipes & tastes that LOVE,

Congratulations, for your life has been touched by
The Loving Chef!

Illa & Jeetu
Certified Tao Master Teachers of Dr & Master Zhi Gang Sha Tao Academy

Who is The Loving Chef ?

Natasha is a Michelin trained, vegan chef, providing healing, nourishing food to Northamptonshire from her farmhouse kitchen.

Based at Sol Haven C.I.C in Moulton, Natasha offers a community farm, and eco therapy for the less advantaged and vulnerable who volunteer on a weekly basis.

She loves to harvest, prepare, cook and serve in the shortest amount of time, therefore offering the most nutrients and flavour in the dishes she prepares.

My heart is filled with so much gratitude

Dearest Beautiful Soul,

With all of my heart, I thank you, for choosing to purchase this book, as you may have gathered this is so much more than just another download or purchase you can place on your phone or shelf. I hope you find it filled with love and greatness.

Each recipe page has a "VIDEO LINK" that you right click so you can cook along with a pre recorded video that was filmed in Veganuary. Each of the videos contains more in depth knowledge and wisdom of many of the ingredients being used and also other uses of different ingredients that you have in your pantry, so you can watch time and time again.

But it goes much deeper than just cooking and watching a video, YOU have also contributed towards making a difference, as YOUR purchase will help fund Sol Haven C.I.C.

The true inspiration within this project is that it fulfils more than just a vision of future potential. By involving people who have very real needs today, it also encapsulates a genuine chance to change lives and build communities.

YOUR PURCHASE – THEIR OPPORTUNITY

Supporting vulnerable people in creating a new life

Thank you thank you thank you

Wishing you

LOVE, PEACE AND HARMONY

Sol Haven

Changing the world one heart at a time . . .

Whether you believe in serendipity, opportunity, setting goals, or the convergence of universal influence, sometimes vision and ideals are just too hard to ignore.

For Sammuel and Natasha, the catalyst was the emerging permaculture movement which began watering seeds that had lived long in their hearts and deserved to see some light.

The farm, the street, and the classroom . . .

The journey that brought these two entrepreneurial visionaries to this point in their lives, though, is far greater than just ecological growing.

Their bigger picture is to explore, develop and create a practical environment where this exciting idea can be used to determine a better today and brighter tomorrow.

They want to improve science and prove the application of its techniques to encourage others to get involved in more projects.

And what's more, they have already demonstrated they are well-able and well-equipped to fulfill this goal.

The true inspiration within this project is that it fulfills more than just a vision of future potential. By involving people who have very real needs today, also encapsulates a genuine chance to change lives and build a community.

From their earliest conversations and excited musings about the project, they were determined that it would be a haven of work and development opportunity for homeless & vulnerable adults experiencing mental health challenges & isolation.

As the scope and potential of the idea has evolved, there are now plans in place to develop learning resources, workshops, wellbeing retreats & cooking classes.

This project is very much a fulfilment of the purpose for Sammuel and Natasha and their personal stories have both fuelled and directed their passion to make it happen.

Surviving several childhood challenges, and battling various addictions in her early life, Natasha experienced being homeless at a young age.

The people that helped her out of those dark places inspired her faith in the love of others and the joy of making a difference.

She vowed to 'give back' and has thrown her efforts behind basket brigades, dinner shelters, gratitude days, and the like ever since.

For Natasha, the farm project is the start of true fulfilment for her life and beyond.

From an early age, Sammuel worked with volunteer groups and communities working with people like the homeless, disabled, people with learning disabilities – even going as far as Africa to work.

Following a traumatic, violent, & emotionally disturbing experience he became homeless while dealing with Post Traumatic Stress and he knew that his life needed healing and sought help through counselling, mediation, dance.

They founded Sol Haven, a Community Permaculture farm, as a way to help enable people to rebuild their lives.

Their experience has successfully shown that being closer to nature and the environment, calms emotions and helps reconnection with oneself and then the outside world.

Their journey a perfect cycle. It is a seemingly coincidental scenario that led them to this point!

They believe it was 'meant to be' and when you see their purpose turning into very real results, it is hard not to come to the same conclusion.

Changing the world one heart at a time . . . from radio, awards, demostrations, retreats and workshops.

Veganlife Live demo   Silverstone Live demo

Table of Contents

1. OAT PORRIDGE
2. QUICK OAT MILK
3. HEMP & CHIA PORRIDGE
4. HOMEMADE GRANOLA
5. NO BAKE OAT & WALNUT COOKIES
6. AVOCADO PROTEIN SHAKE
7. BLACK BEAN & QUINOA SOUP
8. GUACAMOLE DIP
9. VEGAN PASTRY
10. BASIC WHITE SAUCE (BÉCHAMEL)
11. CAULIFLOWER RICE RISOTTO
12. HOT CHOCOLATE
13. SAVOURY RICE
14. TAHINI & AVOCADO DRESSING
15. EGGLESS SPONGE CUPCAKES

16 COCONUT & CHOCOLATE BARS

17 GINGERBREAD BISCOTTI

18 CREAMED SPINACH

19 GLUTEN FREE PANCAKES

20 NUT & BLACK BEAN BURGERS

21 QUICK & EASY HUMMUS

22 HOMEMADE MAYONNAISE

23 CHICKPEA FLOUR CRACKER

24 SPICY VEGETABLE SOUP

25 TOFU PAD THAI

26 COURGETTE & CHOCOLATE CAKE

27 VEGAN MUSHROOM GRAVY

28 SWEET ENERGY BARS

29 FROZEN HERB CUBES

30 CAULIFLOWER BUFFALO BITES

31 BAKED LEMON CHEESECAKE

Oat Porridge

Serves: 2
Prep: 5 mins
Cook: 5 mins

WHAT YOU NEED

- 4 tbsp of flat oats
- 2 tbsp chia seeds
- 250ml / 8fl oz oat milk or any dairy-free milk
- 2 tbsp flaxseed
- handful of dry fruits, nuts, fresh seasonal fruits etc.
- ½ tsp cinnamon powder
- sweetener of choice : maple syrup, date syrup, coconut sugar etc

WHAT YOU NEED TO DO

Put the porridge oats, oat milk, cinnamon, flaxseeds & chia seeds into a saucepan & bring to a gentle simmer.

Add to the porridge, dried fruit, nuts, seeds, seasonal fruits & sweetener to taste.

Keep stirring as it continues cooking until thickened to your desired consistency.

COOKS TIPS

It is important as a vegan to ensure you are getting lots of healthy fats that can be found in nuts & seeds.

Adding chia seeds to porridge adds calcium, omega-3, protein & fibre.

Bananas, berries, apples or peaches would go wonderfully with this recipe.

SCAN THE QR CODE TO WATCH THE VIDEO

www.thelovingchef.co.uk

1
OAT PORRIDGE

2
QUICK OAT MILK

Quick Oat Milk

WHAT YOU NEED

- 100g / 4oz porridge oats
- 750ml / 25fl oz cold water
- sweetener of choice : maple syrup, date syrup, coconut sugar etc (optional)

Makes: 750ml
Prep: 15 mins plus at least 4 hrs soaking

WHAT YOU NEED TO DO

Put the porridge oats in a bowl & cover with filtered water until the oats are submerged. Cover the bowl & leave for 4 hrs or overnight, somewhere cool.

Tip the oats & water into a liquidiser or food processor.

Blend for 2-4 mins until completely smooth, & there are no oats visible.

Line a sieve with a clean piece of muslin or cheesecloth.

Put the lined sieve over a bowl or jug & pour in the oat milk.

Gather the sides of the muslin together & squeeze tightly with both hands to extract the milk.

Add syrup if you prefer a sweeter taste, or add more water if you prefer a thinner consistency.

It will last 3-4 days in a bottle or container placed in the fridge.

www.thelovingchef.co.uk

SCAN THE QR CODE TO WATCH THE VIDEO

Hemp & Chia Porridge

Serves: 2
Prep: 5 mins
Cook: 5 mins

WHAT YOU NEED

- 4 tbsp hulled hemp seeds
- 2 tbs chia seeds
- 2 tbs flaxseed
- 250ml / 8fl oz dairy-free milk or water
- sweetener of choice : maple syrup, date syrup, coconut sugar etc
- handful of dry fruits, nuts, fresh seasonal fruits etc.

WHAT YOU NEED TO DO

In a saucepan over medium heat stir together the oat milk, hemp seeds, chia seeds, flax seeds & sweetener of choice until the mixture begins to bubble.

Add to the porridge, dried fruit, nuts, seeds, seasonal fruits & keep cooking/stirring for 3-4 minutes or until it reaches your favorite texture.

If you prefer a creamy texture give the mixture a quick blend with a hand blender.

Serve immediately with your favourite toppings.

COOKS TIPS

Hemp seeds are an excellent source of Iron, Niacin, Thiamine, Phosphorus, Magnesium, Manganese, Copper, & Zinc.

Add ½ tsp of ginger & all spice plus a clove to the seed mix (while cooking) to create a warming blend of seed porridge.

SCAN THE QR CODE TO WATCH THE VIDEO

www.thelovingchef.co.uk

3
HEMP & CHIA PORRIDGE

4
HOMEMADE GRANOLA

Homemade Granola

Serves: 10
Prep: 15 mins
Cook: 10 mins

WHAT YOU NEED

- 50g / 2oz almond
- 50g / 2oz coconut flakes or desiccated coconut
- 50g / 2oz 50g pecans
- 50g / 2oz 50g walnuts
- 100g / 4oz mixed seeds (I used flaxseed, pumpkin, sunflower & chia seeds)
- 100g / 4oz sultanas, raisins or any dried fruit of your choice
- 2 tsp vanilla extract
- ½ tsp allspice
- ½ tsp ground ginger
- ½ tsp ground cinnamon
- 3 tbsp coconut oil melted

WHAT YOU NEED TO DO

Preheat oven to 350°F/180°C /Gas 4 & line a large baking tray.

Add all the ingredients except the melted coconut oil, into the food processor & blend until it reaches your desired consistency.

Gently heat the coconut oil in a small saucepan then pour over the granola mixture & stir well so everything is coated.

Spread mixture out evenly in a thin layer onto the oven tray.

Cook for 8-10 minutes until golden, crisp & smelling toasted. Remove from oven & leave to cool before serving.

COOKS TIPS

The granola can be stored in an airtight container for up to a month.

Serve with plant based milk, or sprinkle over yogurt with fruit for an instant dessert.

SCAN THE QR CODE TO WATCH THE VIDEO

www.thelovingchef.co.uk

No Bake Oat & Walnut Cookies

Makes: 30
Prep: 20 mins
Freeze: 4 Hours

WHAT YOU NEED

- 240g / 8oz pitted dates
- 115g / 4oz walnuts
- 175g / 6oz rolled oats
- 1 tbsp milled flaxseed (soaked in 2 tbsp water to form a paste)
- 2 tbsp date or maple syrup
- 2 tsp cinnamon or mixed spice
- 1/4 tsp ginger
- 1 tsp vanilla extract

WHAT YOU NEED TO DO

Line a baking sheets with greaseproof paper & set aside.

In a food processor, process dates, walnuts & the oats until a breadcrumb consistency. Be careful not to over-process or they will become too buttery.

Now add the flaxseed paste, date syrup, vanilla & spices. Mix until dough-like (add a tiny amount of water if mixture is too crumbly).

Using a rounded tablespoon, scoop out balls of the cookie mixture, onto the baking tray.

Using your hands press the mixture from the top to flatten them, & shape into a rounded cookie appearance.

Pop them in the refrigerator for about 4 hours to firm up before eating.

SCAN THE QR CODE TO WATCH THE VIDEO

THE LOVING CHEF
www.thelovingchef.co.uk

5
NO BAKE OAT & WALNUT COOKIES

Avocado Protein Shake

WHAT YOU NEED

- 250ml / 8fl oz any dairy-free milk
- 1 medium ripe avocado
- 1 dstspn pea or hemp protein
- 1 tbsp hemp seeds (shelled)
- 1 tbsp cocoa powder
- ½ tbsp flaxseed or linseed
- 1 tbspn pure almond or peanut butter
- 1 tbsp sweetener of choice : maple syrup, date syrup, coconut sugar etc

Serves: 1-2
Prep: 5 mins

WHAT YOU NEED TO DO

Peel the avocado & discard the pit.

Add all ingredients to a blender & blend until completely smooth.

Serve.

COOKS TIPS

Avocado blends well with any fruit & vegetable, so you can always customize with bananas, berries, kale, spinach, mangoes, to enhance the flavor.

Ideally, it's best when you have it fresh, but if you choose to have it later, you can refrigerate for up to 3 days.

www.thelovingchef.co.uk

SCAN THE QR CODE TO WATCH THE VIDEO

Black Bean & Quina Soup

Serves: 4
Prep: 15 mins
Cook: 1 hour

WHAT YOU NEED

- 2 onions, chopped
- 2 medium sweet potatoes, peeled & cut in chunks
- 3 carrots, chopped
- 2 celery stalk, chopped
- 1 bunch kale, stalked & chopped
- 1 (400g) tin black beans, drained
- 90g / 3 oz quinoa
- 2 cloves garlic, minced
- ½ tsp parsley
- ½ tsp basil
- 3 bay leaves
- ½ tsp oregano
- ½ tsp thyme
- ¾ tsp ground coriander
- ½ tbsp whole grain mustard
- 1 tsp coarse ground black pepper
- 1 tsp ground turmeric
- 1 tsp ginger
- 1 tsp cumin
- 2 vegetable stock cubes

WHAT YOU NEED TO DO

Chop onion, sweet potato, carrots, celery, garlic & put in a large soup pot.

Add 850ml/30 fl oz of boiled water, the remaining soup ingredients (except for the kale), to the pot & stir to combine.

Bring up to a simmer; reduce heat to low, cover & cook for about 1 hour. Add the chopped kale, to the pot 10-15 minutes before serving.

COOKS TIPS

Red kidney, pinto, or cannellini beans may be substituted for black beans. The quinoa adds plenty of protein to this soup.

SCAN THE QR CODE TO WATCH THE VIDEO

www.thelovingchef.co.uk

7
BLACK BEAN & QUINOA SOUP

8
GUACAMOLE DIP

Guacamole Dip

WHAT YOU NEED

- 3 ripe avocados
- 1 small onion sliced
- 4 cloves of garlic
- 3 tomatoes sliced into quarters
- 2 tbsp fresh lime juice
- ½ -1 fresh red chilli seeded & chopped (optional)
- 1 tsp parsley
- 1 tsp coriander
- 1 tsp smoked paprika
- salt & pepper to taste

Serves: 8
Prep: 10 mins

WHAT YOU NEED TO DO

Remove the flesh from the avocado - slice in half, remove the seed, & scrape out with a spoon into the food processor.

Add in all the other ingredients & pulse until a smooth mixture to your liking.

Put in a airtight container & chill before use.

COOKS TIPS

To prevent your guacamole from turning brown, always store in an airtight container.

Experiment with the flavors. Maybe add extra chilies if you like a spicier dip, or garlic for added pleasure.

Serve with sliced raw vegetables or flat breads for dipping

www.thelovingchef.co.uk

SCAN THE QR CODE TO WATCH THE VIDEO

Vegan Pastry

Fills: 20cm (8in) Tart pan
Prep: 20 mins
Cook: as per recipe

WHAT YOU NEED

- 200g / 7oz plain flour
- 1 tsp mixed herbs
- ½ tsp salt
- ½ tsp black pepper
- 6 tbsp olive oil
- 3 tbsp ice cold water

WHAT YOU NEED TO DO

Place the flour, salt & mixed herbs into a food processor. Add in olive oil & pulse until the mixture is crumbly & resembles breadcrumbs.

Pour mixture into a bowl.

Gradually stir in cold water & mix gently with a spoon until the mixture forms a dough.

If you press the dough together it needs to stick to itself & not just crumble away. It shouldn't be so sticky that it's sticking to your hands.

If the mixture is not holding together slowly add more water, ½ tbsp at a time. If it's too sticky, add some additional flour 1-2 tbsp at a time.

Shape the dough lightly to form a ball. Put back in bowl or wrap in cling film & allow to rest in the fridge for at least 20 minutes, up to overnight.

SCAN THE QR CODE TO WATCH THE VIDEO

www.thelovingchef.co.uk

9
VEGAN PASTRY

10
VEGAN WHITE SAUCE (BECHAMEL)

Vegan White Sauce (Bechamel)

WHAT YOU NEED

- 4-5 tbsp olive or sunflower oil
- 2 tbsp flour
- 500ml / 18fl oz dairy-free milk
- salt & pepper to taste
- mushrooms /onions (optional)

Serves: 8
Prep: 10 mins

WHAT YOU NEED TO DO

Heat the oil in a pan to medium heat (If adding onions or mushrooms to your sauce, add now & sauté on a low to medium heat until the onion has softened but not coloured & the mushrooms are soft but have not released their juices).

Add flour slowly & whisk to avoid lumps. Reduce heat & let cook together for 2-3 minutes while stirring continuously, being careful not to burn or brown the flour.

Add the milk to the roux gradually, stirring as you go, until you get a smooth sauce. Cook for 5-10 mins, stirring continuously, until the sauce has thickened.

Season to taste.

COOKS TIPS

Whisk & whisk until your arms fall off – this will help you achieve that perfect silky smooth consistency.

Add in some pesto for a creamy herb-filled sauce or stir in nutritional yeast for a cheesy taste.

Use this sauce in classic dishes such as lasagna or moussaka.

SCAN THE QR CODE TO WATCH THE VIDEO

www.thelovingchef.co.uk

Cauliflower Rice Risotto

Serves: 2
Prep: 10 mins
Cook: 20 mins

WHAT YOU NEED

- 1 leek washed & chopped
- 2 carrots chopped
- 1 courgette chopped
- 85 / 3oz mushrooms chopped
- 1 head cauliflower washed, trimmed & grated
- slice of fresh turmeric finely chopped
- 60g / 2oz spinach
- 1 bell pepper cored & chopped
- 4 tbsp nutritional yeast
- 3 cloves garlic finely chopped
- 2 tsp mixed herbs
- 125ml / 4fl oz oat milk
- salt & pepper to taste

WHAT YOU NEED TO DO

Put oil into pan & heat over medium high heat. Add leeks & carrots & cook, stirring occasionally, until soft, about 5 minutes.

Add courgettes, mushrooms, fresh turmeric, garlic & peppers & saute for another 5 minutes. Add in the herbs & oat milk then reduce the heat to medium low.

Using a box grater, grate florets through the medium-sized holes or alternatively use a food processor fitted with a grater attachment.

Add the grated cauliflower to your pan & season with salt & pepper. and nutritional yeast.

Cook the risotto, stirring often for 10-15 minutes, until the cauliflower has softened

Finally add spinach & mix well again allowing it to cook for about 2 more minutes until the spinach has wilted & become shiny. Garnish with fresh chopped parsley & pine nuts if desired & serve warm.

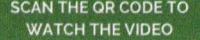

SCAN THE QR CODE TO WATCH THE VIDEO

www.thelovingchef.co.uk

11
CAULIFLOWER RICE RISOTTO

12
HOT CHOCOLATE

Hot Chocolate

WHAT YOU NEED

- 1 cinnamon stick
- 2 cloves
- pinch of chili (optional)
- 650ml dairy-free milk of choice
- ½ tsp sweetener of choice (date syrup, maple or coconut sugar)
- 2 tsp raw cacao / cocoa powder

Serves: 2
Prep: time to marinate milk
Cook: 5 mins

WHAT YOU NEED TO DO

Prepare your milk by adding the cinnamon, cloves, chilli & allow to marinate for a while.

Heat the milk, in a small pan over a low heat, stirring frequently. Add in sweetener of choice.

Whisk the cacao/cocoa powder into a paste with some water. Add the paste to the milk mixture, whisking to combine the cacao with the milk & heat until simmering.

Remove & discard the cloves cinnamon & enjoy immediately.

COOKS TIPS

Cacao is an excellent source of monounsaturated fats, cholesterol-free saturated fats, vitamins, minerals, fiber, natural carbohydrates, & protein that make it an excellent source of nutrients.

Try adding some orange zest in the marinade for that chocolate orange taste.

www.thelovingchef.co.uk

SCAN THE QR CODE TO WATCH THE VIDEO

Savoury Rice

Serves: 4
Prep: 15 mins
Cook: 40 mins

WHAT YOU NEED

- 1 courgette finely chopped
- 2 medium carrots chopped
- 1 leek finely chopped
- 2 celery sticks finely chopped
- 4 tomatoes chopped
- 50g / 2oz frozen peas
- 50g / 2oz sweetcorn
- 268g / 9oz kale
- 2 large bell peppers, cut into chunks,
- 150g mixed seeds (I used pumpkin, linseed & sunflower)
- 2 cloves garlic, chopped
- 2 tsp turmeric
- 1 tsp cumin
- 1 tsp mustard seeds
- 1 tsp smoked paprika
- ½ tsp fennel seeds (optional)
- ½ tsp cardamom seeds
- 300g / 11oz uncooked long grain rice , white or brown
- 710ml / 25fl oz veg stock
- 2 tsp parsley
- 2 tsp coriander
- 2 tbsp vegan nutritional yeast

WHAT YOU NEED TO DO

Preheat oven to 180C/fan 160C/gas 4.

Heat a couple tbsp of oil in a ovenproof saucepan over low heat. Add leek, carrots, celery & fry for about 5 minutes or until the leeks are translucent.

Add in the courgette, spices & seeds, mix well & cook for a further 2 mins stirring occasionally.

Once the vegetables, seeds & nuts start going brown, add in peppers, tomatoes, rice, peas, sweetcorn, vegetable stock, yeast & herbs.

As soon as the liquid on the entire surface is bubbling, give it a good stir, cover the pan with a lid or a sheet of foil, then cook in the oven for 35-40 mins or when the liquid has all been absorbed & the rice is tender.

10 minutes before end of cooking time. add the kale & replace lid.

SCAN THE QR CODE TO WATCH THE VIDEO

www.thelovingchef.co.uk

13
SAVOURY RICE

14
TAHINI & AVOCADO DRESSING

Tahini & Avocado Dressing

WHAT YOU NEED

- 79ml / 3fl oz tahini
- 1 lemon, juiced
- 1 lime, juiced
- 1 tbsp mint
- salt & pepper, to taste
- 1 tsp smoked paprika
- 1 tsp turmeric
- 1 tsp ginger
- 2 cloves garlic crushed
- 1 medium-large avocado, peeled & pitted
- 3-6 tbsp water
- 1-2 tbsp maple syrup

Serves: 4
Prep: 5 mins

WHAT YOU NEED TO DO

Add all ingredients to a blender or food processor.

Blitz until smooth and creamy.

If dressing is too thick, add more water as needed to achieve desired consistency.

Season generously to taste,

COOKS TIPS

Tahini is made by grinding sesame seeds into a smooth paste.

Feel free to replace the mint with any herb or herb blend that you would like.

Enjoy fresh, or store in the refrigerator up to 5 days.

THE LOVING CHEF
www.thelovingchef.co.uk

SCAN THE QR CODE TO WATCH THE VIDEO

Eggless Sponge Cupcakes

Makes: 12
Prep: 15 mins
Cook: 20 mins

WHAT YOU NEED

- 225g / 7oz plain flour
- 125g / 4oz refined white sugar or coconut sugar
- 1 tsp bicarbonate of soda
- 1 tsp salt
- 2 tsp vanilla extract
- 200ml / 7fl oz dairy-free milk
- 80ml / 3fl oz sunflower oil
- 1 tbsp white wine vinegar

WHAT YOU NEED TO DO

Heat the oven to 180C / 160C fan /gas 4.

Line the holes of a 12-hole cupcake tin with paper cases.

Sift flour into a mixing bowl & add sugar, bicarbonate of soda, vanilla extract & salt. Mix together.

Add the milk ,oil & lastly the vinegar to the dry ingredients & whisk until you have a smooth thick batter. (Don't over mix.)

Quickly divide between the cupcake cases, filling them two-thirds full, & bake for 15-20 mins until golden & risen & a toothpick inserted into the center of one of the cakes comes out clean.

Leave to cool on a wire rack.

COOKS TIPS

Don't over stir the cake batter. You don't want to stir out the bubbles.

You can store your cake in an airtight container at room temperature for 3 days or in the fridge for up to 5 days. These cakes are suitable for freezing.

SCAN THE QR CODE TO WATCH THE VIDEO

The Loving Chef
www.thelovingchef.co.uk

15
EGGLESS SPONGE CUPCAKES

16
COCONUT & CHOCOLATE BARS

Coconut & Chocolate Bars

WHAT YOU NEED

- 200g / 7oz desiccated coconut
- 4 tbsp of full fat coconut milk (discard the watery part- if you put the can in the fridge overnight, when you open the can, the fat will have solidified)
- 2 tbsp of maple syrup
- 200g / 7oz organic dark chocolate

Makes: 12
Prep: 10 mins
Chill time: 30 mins

WHAT YOU NEED TO DO

In a food processor add the desiccated coconut, coconut milk & maple syrup.

Mix for 30 seconds or until combined & a moulding consistency.

Shape the mixture into small logs & arrange them on a baking tray covered with grease proof paper.

Refrigerate for 30 mins- 1 hour in the fridge, or in the freezer for 10-15 min.

Melt the chocolate using a glass bowl placed over a pot of boiling water (ensure your bowl isn't touching the water) or carefully in the microwave.

Dip each bar into melted chocolate & arrange on a cooling rack. Sprinkle desiccated coconut on top & allow the bars to set before serving.

Store in the fridge for up to 5 days.

THE LOVING CHEF
www.thelovingchef.co.uk

SCAN THE QR CODE TO WATCH THE VIDEO

Gingerbread Biscotti

Makes: 24
Prep: 30 mins
Cook: 45 mins

WHAT YOU NEED

- 200g / 7oz oats
- 220g / 8oz rye flour
- ¾ tsp cloves (powered or whole)
- 1 tsp ginger
- 1 ½ tsp cinnamon
- 1/2 tsp baking powder
- 1/4 tsp bicarbonate of soda
- 200g / 7oz whole oats
- 177ml / 6fl oz maple syrup
- 177ml / 6fl oz molasses or date syrup
- 1 tsp vanilla essence
- 170g / 6oz raisins

WHAT YOU NEED TO DO

Preheat oven to 350°F/180°C /Gas 4 & line a baking sheet with greaseproof paper.

Add the oats & cloves into a bowl & blend until a flour like consistency.

Add the ginger, cinnamon, baking powder, bicarbonate of soda, rye flour & whole oats, then give it a quick mix to ensure both the baking powder & bicarbonate of soda are equally distributed. Add maple syrup, molasses, vanilla essence & raisins, then mix until a smooth dough forms.

Making sure it is all bonding together, fashion dough into a log shape approx 10 to 12 inches long & 3 to 4 inches wide.

Bake in oven for about 30 minutes or till golden brown & firm to touch.

Carefully slide log onto a cutting board & with a sharp knife, press down firmly & cut slices ½" wide. Gently move slices back to baking sheet & bake again for about 10-15 minutes until slightly toasted; be careful not to burn them.

Allow biscotti to cool 10 minutes on baking sheet, then cool completely on wire racks.

SCAN THE QR CODE TO WATCH THE VIDEO

THE LOVING CHEF
www.thelovingchef.co.uk

17
GINGERBREAD BISCOTTI

18
CREAMED SPINACH

Creamed Spinach

Serves: 4
Prep: 20 mins
Cook: 10 mins

WHAT YOU NEED

- 200g / 7oz fresh or bagged spinach
- 1 small onion, finely chopped
- 1-2 cloves of garlic finely chopped
- 100g / 4oz flour
- 250ml / 9fl oz cashew nut milk
- salt & pepper to taste
- 1 pinch freshly grated nutmeg
- 1 tsp smoked paprika
- 1 tsp nutritional yeast
- 75ml / 3fl oz oat or vegan yogurt (Optional)
- juice of ½ lemon

WHAT YOU NEED TO DO

Put well washed spinach into a pan, cover & steam until the spinach has wilted. It should take less than a minute.

Drain in a colander & squeeze to remove as much liquid from the spinach as possible. Coarsely chop, & set aside.

Add to a frying pan, finely chopped onion & garlic with a little bit of oil or water & gently cook, stirring occasionally, until the onion softens & becomes transparent (3 to 5 minutes.)

Add a little bit of flour & cook for 2 mins, stirring all the time then slowly stir in the cashew milk, black pepper, salt, nutmeg & paprika.

Now add in a little vegan yeast, the yoghurt (optional) & stir until the sauce has thickened.

Add a splash of lemon juice to the mixture, stir in the chopped spinach then serve.

The Loving Chef
www.thelovingchef.co.uk

SCAN THE QR CODE TO WATCH THE VIDEO

Gluten Free Pancakes

Serves: 2-4
Prep: 15 mins
Cook: 10 mins

WHAT YOU NEED

- 325ml / 15fl oz any dairy-free milk
- 250g / 8oz gluten free flour
- 3 tbsp oil,
- 2 tbsp ground flaxseed
- 3 tbsp maple or date syrup
- good pinch salt
- 1 tsp vanilla essence
- 1/2 tsp cinnamon
- 1 tbsp baking powder
- ½ tsp bicarbonate of soda

WHAT YOU NEED TO DO

Put the milk, oil, flaxseed, vanilla essence & maple syrup in a bowl & whisk thoroughly. Now let that sit on the side.

In a large bowl, mix with a whisk, the flour, salt, cinnamon, baking powder, & bicarbonate of soda.

Add the dry ingredients to the wet ingredients & whisk until you get a smooth batter.

Heat about 1/2 tsp oil on a medium/high heat. Wait for the oil to heat up before adding the batter.

Add 1-2 tbsp of the batter to make each pancake. Cook for about a minute, or until bubbles are popping on the surface & just the edges look dry & slightly shiny.

Pop a spatula under an edge to see how it's coming along underneath.

Once golden brown on the underside, flip it over & cook the other side until also golden brown .

Transfer to a plate & keep warm while you cook the rest.

SCAN THE QR CODE TO WATCH THE VIDEO

The Loving Chef
www.thelovingchef.co.uk

19
GLUTEN FREE PANCAKES

20
NUT & BLACK BEAN BURGERS

Nut & Black Bean Burgers

WHAT YOU NEED

- 50g / 2oz ground flaxseed
- 1 tsp lemon juice
- 75g / 3oz oats
- 400g canned black beans
- 175g / 6oz nuts (any you like)
- 1 medium onion, finely chopped
- 3 cloves of garlic chopped
- 1/2 tsp turmeric
- 2 tbsp tahini
- 1 tsp vegan nutritional yeast
- 1 tsp paprika
- 25g / 1oz parsley
- 2 tsp brown rice miso

Serves: 4
Prep: 15 mins
Cook: 50 mins

WHAT YOU NEED TO DO

Add the flaxseed to a bowl along with the lemon juice & let this sit for 5-10 minutes while preparing the rest of the ingredients.

In a food processor, add the oats & pulse until a flour like consistency.

Add the black beans, nuts, onion, garlic & turmeric & pulse repeatedly until everything is chopped down to a coarse paste.

Now add the tahini, yeast, paprika, parsley, brown rice miso & flaxseed mixture to the food processor & blend until combined, but not smooth – you want to retain a bit of texture.

Divide & shape the mixture into equal-sized patties, place an a baking tray covered in parchment paper & let them rest for at least 30 mins in the fridge.

Heat a splash of oil in a large frying pan over a medium heat, add the patties & cook for 10 minutes, or until golden & cooked through, turning halfway.

or

Bake at 350° F/180°C for about 30 minutes on one side, then flip & bake for another 20 minutes (your times may vary).

Delicious served with a fresh green salad.

THE LOVING CHEF
FOOD FOR YOUR SOUL
www.thelovingchef.co.uk

SCAN THE QR CODE TO WATCH THE VIDEO

Quick & Easy Hummus

Makes: 300ml
Prep: 15 mins

WHAT YOU NEED

- 1 425g / 15oz can chickpeas drained
- 1-2 garlic cloves
- juice of 1 or 2 lemons
- generous pinch of salt & pepper to taste
- ½ tsp paprika
- 2 tbsp oil
- 4 tbsp tahini

WHAT YOU NEED TO DO

Place chickpeas, garlic, tahini, lemon juice, pepper, salt, paprika & oil into a food processor.

Process for about 1 minute or until the hummus is smooth & silky.

Hummus can be served straight away however it will taste even better if covered & refrigerated for at least 30 minutes before serving.

COOKS TIPS

If using dried chickpeas soak, boil & use when cool.

If you like a thinner hummus add water or leftover liquid from the can of chickpeas a little at a time, until you have reached the desired consistency.

Homemade hummus stored in an airtight container should last for up to 3-4 days in the refrigerator.

SCAN THE QR CODE TO WATCH THE VIDEO

The Loving Chef
www.thelovingchef.co.uk

21
QUICK & EASY HUMMUS

22
HOME MADE MAYONNAISE

Home Made Mayonnaise

WHAT YOU NEED

- 3 tbsp aquafaba (tinned bean water from chickpeas, butter beans or cannellini beans)
- ¾ tsp salt
- 2 tsp Dijon mustard
- 2 tbsp apple cider vinegar
- 1 tbsp maple syrup
- 250ml/ 9fl oz sunflower oil

Makes: 300ml
Prep: 5 mins

WHAT YOU NEED TO DO

Measure the aquafaba, salt, mustard, vinegar & maple syrup in a jug.

Give a quick whizz with a hand blender to mix everything up & the aquafaba is looking foamy.

With the hand blender running slowly, add the oil in small increments.

Keep drizzling the oil & blending until the mixture is thick & looks like mayo.

Taste & add more cider vinegar if you like a slightly sharper mayo. Similarly, add a bit more mustard &/or salt if preferred.

COOKS TIPS

Keep the hand blender under the liquid to avoid spattering.

Store in a clean jar with lid & keep in the fridge. It should keep for at least a week - cider vinegar is a natural preservative.

THE LOVING CHEF
www.thelovingchef.co.uk

SCAN THE QR CODE TO WATCH THE VIDEO

Chickpea Flour Crackers

Makes: 30
Prep: 15 mins
Cook: 15 mins

WHAT YOU NEED

- 250g / 9oz chickpea/gram flour
- ½ tsp baking powder
- 2 tsp black pepper
- 2 tsp salt
- 125ml / 4fl oz water
- 1 tsp olive oil
- topping - sesame seeds, rosemary or chillies

WHAT YOU NEED TO DO

Preheat the oven to 350 F/180°C /Gas 4 & line a baking tray with greaseproof paper.

In a bowl add your dry ingredients mix, add 1 teaspoon of olive oil, & mix again.

Slowly add water until you form a pastry like consistency. Mix until the dough is uniform & comes together.

Roll into a ball, sprinkle surface with flour, flatten, & roll out as thin as possible. You can use your hands to flatten or a rolling pin.

Onto the surface of your pastry, sprinkle sesame seeds, rosemary or chillies & a pinch of salt (use the salt sparingly) & lightly roll over with your rolling pin.

Cut into desired shapes.

Put onto tray & bake in the oven for about 10-15 minutes (until they are lightly golden and crispy)

Enjoy as a healthy, gluten free snack or accompaniment to dinner.

SCAN THE QR CODE TO WATCH THE VIDEO

The Loving Chef
www.thelovingchef.co.uk

23
CHICKPEA FLOUR CRACKERS

24
SPICY VEGETABLE SOUP

Spicy Vegetable Soup

WHAT YOU NEED

- 800g / 2lbs root veg (carrot, parsnip, turnip etc)
- 2 onion roughly chopped
- 2 tsp olive oil
- 2 bay leaves
- 1 tsp cumin
- 1 tsp cardamom seeds
- 2 garlic cloves, thinly sliced
- 1 tsp cinnamon
- 1 tsp cayenne pepper
- 1 tsp turmeric
- 1 tsp ginger
- salt & pepper to taste

Serves: 4
Prep: 20 mins
Cook: 30 mins

WHAT YOU NEED TO DO

Heat oil in a large pot & gently fry the onions for 6–8 minutes, until softened & beginning to brown.

Peel & chop the root vegetables into cubes, add the chunks to your pot & cook for 5 minutes more, stirring occasionally. Stir in the garlic & cook for a few seconds more.

Add 1 litre/1¾ pints water, all the spices, salt & pepper. Stir well & bring to the boil.

Reduce the heat to a simmer, cover the pan loosely with a lid & cook for about 20 minutes or until the vegetables are very soft, stirring occasionally.

COOKS TIPS

You can use any hard, root vegetables you like for this simple soup. Carrots, parsnips, sweet potatoes, squash, beetroot & celeriac all work well.

The smaller you chop the pieces, the faster they will cook.

THE LOVING CHEF
www.thelovingchef.co.uk

SCAN THE QR CODE TO WATCH THE VIDEO

Tofu Pad Thai

Serves: 4
Prep: 15 mins
Cook: 15 mins

WHAT YOU NEED

- 2 carrots
- 3 spring onion
- 3 garlic cloves chopped
- Turmeric
- 300g / 11oz tofu
- 1 tbsp chopped ginger
- 1 courgette
- 1 pepper
- 100g / 4 oz mushrooms
- Juice of 2 limes
- 2 tbsp peanut butter
- 1 vegetable stock cube
- 1 bunch kale (about 10 ounces), steamed & washed
- 64g / 2oz frozen peas
- 200g / 7oz rice noodles

WHAT YOU NEED TO DO

Cook the rice noodles according to package instructions. Optional: You can add one tablespoon of oil to water. It prevents noodles from sticking to one another.

Once cooked, immediately rinse in cold water & set aside.

Wash & prepare the vegetables & thinly slice to a similar size. Drain the tofu & cut into small cubes.

Heat a large frying pan over a medium heat. Add 1 tsp olive oil, sliced carrots & cook for a couple of minutes giving it a occasional stir. Now add finely chopped garlic, turmeric, ginger & tofu. Stir fry for a few minutes.

Add the rest of your vegetables except the kale & peas (these cook really fast & should be added towards the end when other vegetables are almost cooked).

Stir fry for a further few more minutes. Finally add the lime juice, peanut butter, stock cube, peas & kale. Mix to coat the vegetables with the sauce & cook for 2-3 minutes.

Stir in the cooked rice noodles & mix well with the vegetables & sauce. Enjoy immediately.

SCAN THE QR CODE TO WATCH THE VIDEO

THE LOVING CHEF
www.thelovingchef.co.uk

25
TOFU PAD THAI

26
COURGETTE & CHOCOLATE CAKE

Courgette & Chocolate Cake

WHAT YOU NEED

- 260g / 9oz almond butter
- 60ml / 2fl oz maple syrup
- 1 and half banana mashed
- 250g / 9oz grated courgette (about 2 medium-sized)
- 50g / 1oz cocoa powder
- 100g vegan chocolate broken up
- 1 tsp ground cinnamon
- pinch of salt
- 2 tsp vanilla essence
- 1 tsp baking powder
- A tangy sharp sauce to serve with it.

Serves: 10
Prep: 10 mins
Cook: 40mins

WHAT YOU NEED TO DO

Preheat the oven to 180°C/350°F /Gas 4.

Grease a non-stick spring form cake tin. Line bottom of tin with grease proof paper. we use a 9 inch tin but a small tin the thicker the cake will become (cooking time may need to be adjusted)

In a large bowl add almond butter, maple syrup, banana & mix well.

Add cocoa powder, cinnamon, salt, vanilla essence, broken chocolate (keep some aside to sprinkle on top), grated courgettes & mix until all is well combined.

Now add the baking powder & give it a quick mix again.

Pour into the baking tin. Sprinkle the top with some more broken chocolate.

Bake for 35-40 minutes or until a skewer inserted comes out clean.

Leave the cake to cool in the tin for 10 minutes & then turn out onto a cooling rack.

Serve with a tangy sharp sauce i.e. Blueberry, Blackberry, Black Cherry.

THE LOVING CHEF
FOOD FOR YOUR SOUL
www.thelovingchef.co.uk

SCAN THE QR CODE TO WATCH THE VIDEO

Vegan Mushroom Gravy

Serves: 6
Prep: 10 mins
Cook: 10 mins

WHAT YOU NEED

- 1oz dried porcini mushrooms (soaked for 30 mins -1 hour)
- 500ml /8fl oz water or veg stock
- 1 onion chopped
- 1 tbsp olive oil
- 1 clove garlic, peeled & crushed
- 3 sprigs rosemary chopped
- large handful fresh thyme chopped
- black pepper to taste
- 1 tbsp Dijon mustard
- 2 tbsp corn starch or plain flour

WHAT YOU NEED TO DO

In a small bowl, combine the dried mushrooms & water/stock. Let it soak for 30 mins -1 hour.

Heat oil in a saucepan over a medium-high heat. add onions & garlic. Sauté for about 3 minutes until it becomes translucent.

Add thyme, rosemary & mustard. Season with black pepper.

Add cornstarch/flour & mix until flour is completely incorporated.

Gradually add the mushrooms (including the water they were soaked in) stirring well & bring to a boil. Simmer for roughly 10 minutes (or to your desired consistency).

COOKS TIPS

Add fresh mushrooms if you would like.

Marvelous over mashed potatoes, rice or vegan roasts. Leftover gravy can be stored in an airtight container in the fridge for a few days.

SCAN THE QR CODE TO WATCH THE VIDEO

The Loving Chef
www.thelovingchef.co.uk

27
VEGAN MUSHROOM GRAVY

28
SWEET ENERGY BARS

Sweet Energy Bars

WHAT YOU NEED

- 220g / 8oz chopped dates
- 85g / 3oz oats
- 150g / 5oz pecan nuts
- 2 tbsp chia seeds
- 2 tsp cinnamon
- vanilla essence

Makes: 10 Bars
Prep: 15 mins
Cook: 30 mins

WHAT YOU NEED TO DO

Preheat oven to 190°C/374°F /gas 5

Place all your ingredients in a food processor & pulse until small bits remain & it forms a "dough" like consistency that sticks together.

Press mixture firmly into a 7" x 7" baking tin or similar small tin making sure its compact & uniformly flattened.

Pre cut into bars, as this will prevent the bars falling apart when you get out them out of the tin later.

Bake for about 30 minutes.

Remove from the oven & leave to cool completely. The energy bars might crumble if you try to remove them from the tin before they have cooled completely.

COOKS TIPS

Adding a little water to the dates will help soften them up a bit if needed.

Use something flat, like a drinking glass, to press the mixture down compact, will help them hold together better.

Store in an airtight container for up to a few days.

THE LOVING CHEF
www.thelovingchef.co.uk

SCAN THE QR CODE TO WATCH THE VIDEO

Frozen Herb Cubes

Prep: 15 mins

WHAT YOU NEED

- Herb(s) of choice (basil, chives, fennel, lovage, mint, oregano, parsley, rosemary, sage, tarragon, thyme, etc)
- Water
- Ice cube tray

WHAT YOU NEED TO DO

Chop up herb(s) of choice.

Fill each section of an ice cube tray about 3/4 of the way with chopped herbs, compacting firmly.

Top up each section with water.

Freeze until the cubes are frozen solid.

Once ice cubes are frozen, pop them out of their tray & into freezer bags for storage.

Use as needed.

COOKS TIPS

Using a silicone ice cube tray to makes these is highly recommended but any type of Ice tray will work.

Frozen herbs are already chopped & ready to go, so no time is wasted picking herbs off stems & cutting up when in a rush to start cooking

SCAN THE QR CODE TO WATCH THE VIDEO

THE LOVING CHEF
www.thelovingchef.co.uk

29
FROZEN HERB CUBES

30 CAULIFLOWER BUFFALO BITES

Cauliflower Buffalo Bites

WHAT YOU NEED

- 1 large cauliflower, broken into florets
- 125g / 4oz chickpea flour
- 1 tbsp vegan nutritional yeast
- 100ml/ 4fl oz water
- ¼ tsp black pepper
- ¼ tsp salt
- ½ tsp mild curry powder
- ½ tsp paprika
- ½ tsp mixed herbs

Serves: 2
Prep: 10 mins
Cook: 20 mins

WHAT YOU NEED TO DO

Preheat your oven to 210°C/428°F/ gas 7.

Cut the cauliflower head into bite sized pieces/florets.

Put the flour, yeast, curry powder, paprika, salt, black pepper & mixed herbs into a bowl.

Slowly whisk in water until the batter is thick & able to coat the cauliflower nicely.

Dip the cauliflower in the mix ensuring its well covered. This can be done individually or in batches.

Shake off any excess & spread the cauliflower pieces over a lined baking tray in a single layer.

Bake for 20 minutes in the middle of the oven, until golden brown, turning the florets halfway so all sides get golden brown and crispy.

THE LOVING CHEF
www.thelovingchef.co.uk

SCAN THE QR CODE TO WATCH THE VIDEO

Baked Lemon Cheesecake

Serves: 9
Prep: 10 mins
Cook: 60 mins

WHAT YOU NEED

BASE
- 84g / 3oz raw almonds
- 67g / 2oz oats
- 3 tbsp coconut oil
- 118ml / 4fl oz maple syrup
- 118ml / 4fl oz any dairy-free milk

FILLING
- 300g / 11oz cashews nuts (soaked in boiling water for 1 hour)
- 175g / 6oz chickpeas- peeled
- 1 lemon, zested & juiced
- 120ml / 5fl oz maple syrup
- 1 tsp vanilla essence
- 7g / ½ oz arrowroot or corn starch
- 2 tbsp tahini
- 400ml / 14fl oz full fat coconut milk
- 3 tbsp apple cider vinegar
- pinch of salt

WHAT YOU NEED TO DO

Preheat oven to 325°F/160°C /gas 3.

Grease & line a 9 inch round springform tin with greaseproof paper (line both the bottom & the sides).

Add oats, almonds & coconut oil to a food processor & mix on high until a fine meal is achieved.

Add the maple syrup & water & pulse/mix on low until a loose dough is formed, scraping down sides as needed. You should be able to squeeze the mixture between two fingers & form a dough instead of it crumbling. Tip mixture into the cake tin & press evenly into bottom & up the sides.

Drain the cashews & tip into the cleaned out food processor along with all the remaining topping ingredients. Blend on high until very creamy & smooth. Pour filling over the base & spread into an even layer smoothing the top.

Place in the oven & bake for 55-60 minutes, until the filling is firm & lightly golden.

Let rest for 10 minutes at room temperature, then transfer to refrigerator to let cool completely (uncovered). Once cooled, cover & continue refrigerating for 5-6 hours, preferably overnight.

SCAN THE QR CODE TO WATCH THE VIDEO

The Loving Chef
www.thelovingchef.co.uk

31
BAKED LEMON CHEESECAKE

JOIN OUR MEMBERSHIP SITE

Gain **LIFE TIME ACCESS** to our Membership Site (which we are constantly updating) where you will find recipes, videos, tips, tricks, helpful information, community, support and so much more.

Get our 31 Recipe and Video Collection with an accompanying downloadable ebook so you can cook along with Natasha and create healthy, tasty, simple vegan meals not only for yourself but also for family and friends to enjoy.

ENROL TODAY

@NATASHATHELOVINGCHEF | WWW.THELOVINGCHEF.CO.UK

What we care about

1. Earth Care

We believe in the intrinsic value of life. We are committed to regenerating ruined and/or dying landscapes. We allow healthy ecosystems to thrive. We aim to reduce our impact on the environment with zero-waste living. The objective of our project is to bring healing while connecting with mother earth using the best of natural resources and reusing waste to reduce impact on the environment.

2. People Care

We believe in the intrinsic value of humanity. We work to meet peoples' needs of food, shelter, education, and joy. We use a simple step by step processes and systems within a safe working environment to enable to individuals learn, grow and blossom to their full potential.

3. Fair Share

We share our resources to create the best impact on the earth and all its people. This project helps Improve liveability by improving the living environment for communities and reduces the amount of waste produced.

Would you like to spend time with Natasha face to face?

The Loving Chef offers
The Four Seasons to Inner Peace Retreat
Spending 5 days together
The retreat is about wellness for the joy of it. A retreat to learn, cook, balance, de stress and to Nurture in the Spring,
Flow into Summer,
To relax and rest in Autumn,
And embrace a Winter Transformation.

We have a beautiful week planned of creating and making healthy, nutritional, delicious plant-based food, that is wholesome and unprocessed.

You will immerse yourself in connecting deeper as we offer a daily 2 hour sessions and discover The Art of being perfectly imperfect
- finding the true you,

We have an evening offering a Wimhof experience, filled with breathe, ice and fire to move you deep into the subconscious mind to clear trauma and install positive feedback. moving deeply into relaxation & grounded presence!

You will be offered the chance to experience combinations of meditations and gentle movement to balance and attune with one's own body.

The Retreat is only offered 4 times a year
and is inclusive for an intimate group of up to 8 people at a time
so you can dive deep into transformation on a personal level.

If you would like to know more information
please do connect with Natasha directly on
01604 307783
natasha@thelovingchef.co.uk

Here is what others say about their experince with Natasha......

The loving chef is absolutely amazing, high vibrational and delicious food. just spent an amazing weekend at the retreat yurt which was catered by the wonderful natasha. every mouthful was totally yummy and the cakes were heaven
~ AH

Natasha hosted a group of 8 of us, in her yurt in Moulton,
preparing the most delicious and healthy 3 course meal.
It was a celebration with a difference and can't recommend our host, her food and the setting highly enough. There were fairy lights around, and the most glorious sunset right outside the door to the yurt. We felt really privileged to have the place to ourselves, and in my view,
Natasha rightly earns
her title, 'the Loving Chef' in all ways.
~ SG

Natasha was the caterer for my birthday party with 70 people attending. The food was amazing and everyone commented on how fabulous the food was. Right from the start Natasha was friendly, approachable and willing to take an idea and run with it. The food on the night exceeded my expectations and my friends have already asked for her contact details. If you are thinking of booking her don't hesitate and just book - you won't regret it!
~JH

what others say about their experince with Natasha......

I have attended two of Natasha's vegan cookery courses, the two day masterclass, and the one day baking class.
The masterclass expanded my knowledge of vegan food, both raw and cooked, it's nutritional values and potential to support our health. The baking day served up a variety of delicious treats that tasted wonderful without relying on refined sugar.

Natasha has a wonderful teaching style that brings JOY into food and cooking. Her gratitude and personal experience make the days such a positive experience filled with community cooking and sharing, something that is missing so often in today's society.
I would thoroughly recommend both of these courses, and look forward to attending more in the future. ~ KH

Share with us !

We would love you to share your kitchen creation photos and all that you take from the book with us on social media.

Here's how to find us
natashathelovingchef

and if you would like to join The loving Chef Comminuty, Natasha would love to welcome you ~ here's how to find her in facebook

TLC Community

Natasha shares recipes, videos and exclusive offers,
this is where you can get in touch with her, have 1-2-1 or group conversations with her, as well as her sharing knowledge and wisdom as well as getting to know other like minded people.

natasha@thelovingchef.co.uk
Sol Haven, New Manor Farm, Moulton, Northampton,
NN3 7RB
01604 307783

Space for your own notes

Space for your own notes

Printed in Great Britain
by Amazon